FLEA MARKET *Style*

Ideas & Projects for Your World

JERRI FARRIS AND TIM HIMSEL

CREATIVE
PUBLISHING
international

MINNETONKA, MINNESOTA

www.creativepub.com

C ONTENTS

PROJECTS

$\mathcal{P}$REFACE

Flea market style—furnishing your home with found objects—is more than a way of decorating, it's a way of life. It's a decision to live surrounded by stories; sometimes our own, but also those of people we have never known—stories we imagine based on the evidence of living and loving etched into their possessions.

The spirit of flea market style lies in embracing the less-than-perfect, in accepting that the price of being well-loved and well-used is bearing some signs of wear and tear. In her wonderful song, "Heroes," Ann Reed tells us that it's the imperfections that make us whole. And in Margery Williams' ageless children's book, *The Velveteen Rabbit*, the only way to become Real is to be loved into shabbiness.

Flea-market-style homes are Real. That's not to say they're unkempt or untidy—far from it. Part of their charm is the paradox of worn finishes against fresh fabrics, age-softened edges against crisp backgrounds, weathered metal against gleaming crystal accents.

Those of us who love flea market style learn to see things for what they could be as well as for what they are. I've heard it said that Michelangelo believed that his true calling as a sculptor was to reveal the figure waiting within the block of stone. It's something like that for us: An old door holds within it the possibilities of a mirrored plant stand; a stack of mismatched teacups waits to be transformed into a lamp; salvaged lumber reaches out to frame a family photo.

Tim Himsel and Jerri Farris

Although I've always cherished old family pieces, I've only been living flea market style for about ten years. A friend introduced me to my first flea market, Gold Rush Days, in Oronoco, Minnesota. One afternoon of wandering among acres of treasures was all it took—I was hooked for life. Now my home is a welter of the unique and the unusual, gathered over time, loved as is or adapted to new purposes.

I've considered myself a writer since I was eleven years old. While reading *Little Women*, I decided to be Jo, and I've been observing and describing the world around me from that day to this. As a writer and a lover of flea markets, I suppose it was inevitable that I'd find my way to this book. Like the figure in the stone, it's been waiting within me, but it could not have been revealed without my friend and creative partner, the incomparable Tim Himsel.

A graphics artist and creative director, Tim designed the look of the book as well as many of the projects. His talent, imagination, and creativity are reflected on every single page. Tim has a knack for turning our wildest ideas into achievable realities. As you'll find in the stories that follow, he grew up on a farm in southern Wisconsin. I think his mechanical abilities were honed on the farm, where nothing was wasted and machinery and equipment was repaired and adapted year after year. His artistic abilities, on the other hand, are pure gift. On both counts, I'm grateful for the opportunity to work with Tim and learn from him.

Tim and I are privileged to work with a talented, generous group of people, and together we created something no one of us could have done alone. We'd especially like to thank Terrie Myers, Paul Gorton, Dan Widerski, Julie Caruso, John Rajtar, and Tate Carlson, who helped design, build, and photograph the projects.

Jerri Farris

$\mathcal{I}$NTRODUCTION

What exactly is Flea Market Style?

Well, it's not easily defined. It's a style that forges a connection between the best of the past and the present, encompassing a mixture of things—old and new, family heirlooms and found treasures, patterned and plain, textured and shiny. Some elements may be rare or exotic while others are simple and inexpensive. The common threads—significance and beauty—can be found in the eye and heart of the beholder.

Flea market style follows the advice of William Morris, an English designer and the founder of the Arts and Crafts movement, who suggested that we have nothing in our homes that we do not know to be useful and believe to be beautiful.

A home decorated in flea market style is filled with the comfort and atmosphere that can only be provided by well-loved furnishings collected over time. It's not an instant soup, just-add-hot-water kind of style. It takes time and care and imagination to gather the right pieces and use each to its best advantage. Sometimes family heirlooms are used or displayed just as they have been for generations. Other times, a found treasure is altered to give it new life or purpose.

More than anything else, a flea-market-style home is uniquely personal. It may be spare and monochromatic or kitschy and colorful; its theme may be southwestern or northeastern or midwestern farmhouse chic. But no matter what else it may be, it is a home that speaks to the hearts and about the souls of those who live in it.

With flea market style, there's really only one rule: If you love it, it works. The goal here is to create well-appointed rooms that provide a sense of welcome and comfort and enduring grace.

Like charity, flea market style begins at home. Start by looking through your own attic, basement, garage, and storage areas. Are there items that could be refurbished or adapted to another use? Have you stored away things that are "too good" to use every day? Get them out. *Now.* Nothing is too good to be used and enjoyed.

And remember, not everyone recognizes the value of what we consider treasures. Tell people about your interest in old things and volunteer to help clean out storage areas any time you get the chance. You never know what might turn up in someone's attic or basement during spring cleaning or when they're packing to move.

For most flea market fanatics, life is sort of an ongoing treasure hunt. Not only flea markets, but also garage sales, church bazaars, antique stores, live and on-line auctions, and architectural salvage stores can be gold mines. The internet is another valuable resource. Typing the words "flea market" into a search engine will bring up nearly a million sites, and a quick scan will turn up plenty of show listings and on-line markets.

I still prefer the fun of hunting through booths or stalls in person, but if you have your heart set on a specific collectible or unique piece, the vast reach of the internet may be the quickest, easiest way to track it down. Just be sure you're dealing with reputable people and that you're paying a realistic price. On-line sites may provide the easiest way to find something, but they can be expensive places to shop if you're not well informed.

- DRESS COMFORTABLY, IN LAYERS IF THE WEATHER COULD BE VARIABLE. PACK A SMALL BACKPACK WITH SUNGLASSES, A HAT, BOTTLED WATER, AND SUNBLOCK.
- BRING CASH IN SMALL DENOMINATIONS. MANY DEALERS ACCEPT CHECKS OR EVEN CREDIT CARDS, BUT IT'S ALMOST ALWAYS EASIER TO GET THE BEST PRICE IF YOU'RE OFFERING CASH.
- BRING ROOM DIMENSIONS (IF YOU'RE SHOPPING FOR FURNITURE), A TAPE MEASURE, A SMALL NOTEBOOK, AND A PEN.
- IF YOU'RE LOOKING FOR COLLECTIBLES, BRING APPROPRIATE PRICE GUIDES, A MAGNIFYING GLASS, AND A SMALL FLASHLIGHT.
- BRING THE LARGEST VEHICLE YOU HAVE, AND STOCK IT WITH BOXES OR BAGS, PADDING, AND STRING, ROPE, OR BUNGEE CORDS.

My friend, Deb Karnes, introduced me to flea markets and showed me the ropes. You'll find some of her game-day advice in the box at the left.

If you're a beginner and don't have a friend like Deb, go to a book store or library—you'll find flea market guides that list events across the country. You'll also find listings in many regional papers and trade journals. You'll quickly discover that some markets operate every week, year-round; some have schedules that change with the seasons; and others take place only two or three times each year. Pick a couple of likely spots and make some plans! It may be as simple as meeting friends across town on a Saturday morning or as complex as a cross-country road trip.

Before you start shopping, make one more stop at the bookstore or library. Especially if you're in the market for collectibles, it's a good idea to pick up a reliable price guide and study it. You should also look through a couple of books that discuss how to evaluate the age and condition of antiques and primitives. Armed with that kind of information, you're less likely to pay too much for a piece or to pass up the deal of a lifetime.

When you've done your research and picked your targets, you're ready to shop. Let the fun begin!

Experienced flea market fanatics usually start early and stay late or come back at the end of the show. I have to get there early because I'm afraid someone else will get to the treasures before I do. Truly, the early hours often are the time when dealers and professional pickers are combing the booths for the best pieces or trendiest merchandise. At the end of the show, if the piece you want is still available, you might be able to get a better price from a weary dealer who doesn't want to pack it back up. One word of advice: If you absolutely love it, don't walk away. I've never regretted a single thing I've bought, but I still kick myself over a few pieces that got away.

When you first get started, everything in every display will draw your attention, and it will take a long time to move from booth to booth. But after a while, you'll figure out the types of pieces that interest you most and how to spot the dealers who are likely to offer them. Sometimes a quick scan of a booth tells all, and other times you'll need to dig under layers of extraneous bits and pieces to find the treasures waiting there. Follow your instincts—they'll lead you to the good stuff.

Right: When I look at a piece like this, my first thought is, "I could do that!" The big question is not whether you can, but whether you will. If you're like me, the "To Do" list is longer than several lifetimes: Don't walk away from something you truly love.

Bottom left: This little iron piece fairly screams with possibilities. This is the kind of piece I like to keep on hand—it will be the perfect touch for a project some day.

Bottom right: The obvious signs of use on this ladder captured my imagination and its simple construction intrigued Tim. When Tim and I shop, we often find construction details that we later put to use.

When you get the chance, talk with the dealers. Some of them are full of useful information and quite willing to share their knowledge and enthusiasm. When you find a piece you're interested in, ask about its history. Dealers don't always know the origins of their merchandise, but occasionally they have fascinating tales to tell.

If you're a bargain hunter at heart, you probably have your own style of negotiating. If not, practice this phrase: "Is this the best you can do?" Or, try this one: "Can you do better?" These are standard ways of asking for a lower price, and dealers will often come down 10% or so in reply. If you need to, step out of view and consult your trusty pricing guide. Be reasonable, though. You don't want to pay too much, but you don't want to insult a dealer to the point that he or she won't negotiate, either.

Unless you're trained and experienced, you should be searching the flea markets for personal treasures, not investments. With the proliferation of information on the internet and in books, it's very rare to come across a dealer who isn't fully aware of the market value of a piece, but it could happen. If it does, be cautious, act natural, and take your time. As long as you have it in your hands, no one else will buy it.

Before you make a final decision, carefully check the item's condition. Look for signs of damage, repair, or alteration. It may not matter to you, but that should be a decision rather than an oversight. For one thing, you don't want to pay the price for a piece in mint condition if it's actually cracked or the hardware has been replaced.

Above all, be guided by your heart. If something speaks to you, listen. If you absolutely love a piece, you *will* find a place and it *will* work with the other things in the space you make for it. If you feel yourself settling for something that's merely acceptable, walk away. Your rooms won't come together overnight, but when they do, it will be magic.

Marsha Holdhusen, proprietor of
Crescent Moon in St. Paul, Minnesota,
found a way to live out her passion for
unique old things. A psychiatric nurse
who felt she needed a career change,
Marsha took a leap and opened her
shop. Her best advice on flea market
style: "Don't be afraid to mix things up.
You can always make changes later if
you find you don't like them."

$\mathcal{T}$ECHNIQUES

My dear friend Catherine once described her mother as a master at turning candlesticks into lamps and lamps into candlesticks. While this is probably not a skill you aspire to, we hope this book lights your creative fires and inspires you to make use of old materials in new ways.

As we were designing projects and deciding how to describe construction processes, our main goal was to make sure everyday people could actually do the things we suggested. As you look through these pages, we hope you'll think, "Hey! I can do that."

By and large, the techniques necessary for these projects are a matter of common sense. Still, it's useful to think about the best ways to clean vintage fabrics or maintain worn finishes, for example, before you make a mistake that can't be undone. And lamp wiring—though extremely simple—may be something you've never attempted before. No problem. In the next few pages, you'll find ideas and suggestions that will help you clean, maintain, and transform your treasures.

If a project requires tools or materials you haven't used before, take some time to become familiar with them. If it's possible, practice with scrap materials before you start work on the project—it will be worth your time.

If you have questions, most hardware stores or home centers have staff members who are happy to answer questions. If you're still having trouble, write to us at Creative Publishing, international, 5900 Green Oak Drive, Minnetonka, MN 55343 or at DIY@creativepub.com. We love hearing from people who are bringing our ideas to life, and we especially love to see pictures of your creations.

Relax. Have fun. You really can do this.

GETTING STARTED

When you get your treasures home, cleaning and repairing them usually is the first order of the day. Not so fast! Original finishes add enormously to the value of a piece, and even aggressive cleaning can damage them. Certain types of repairs can drastically reduce the value of antiques. It's easy to alter an item and impossible to return it to its original condition, so think carefully before you act. Consult an expert if you have doubts or questions. If you bought the piece from a knowledgeable antiques dealer, start there. If you have reason to believe the piece might be especially valuable, talk to an appraiser or a conservator.

Throughout this chapter, we're going to talk about the kinds of materials we use in the projects to come—old doors, wood chairs, chests or cabinets—run-of-the-mill flea market finds that have appeal based on their character rather than their historical or monetary value. We'll show you how to clean, repair, and adapt items such as these. If you've decided to refinish or restore an antique, first do some research. Bookstores and libraries offer many fine books on the subject.

CLEANING PAINTED FINISHES

Note: Paint from before 1978 is very likely to contain lead. If you suspect you're dealing with lead paint, use proper precautions, and by all means, keep these pieces well out of the reach of children.

Wash painted surfaces with a solution of equal parts of vinegar and water, and a soft cloth; remove flaking paint. To remove stubborn stains, rub the surface gently with a scouring pad; use an old toothbrush in small areas.

Popular opinion seems to be divided about waxing painted pieces. Some experts recommend it and others advise against the idea. I'm not an expert, but I've waxed many painted pieces and have never had a reason to regret it. If you decide to wax a painted surface, use beeswax and a light touch. With a soft, lint-free cloth, rub the wax onto the surface; buff the wax with a clean cloth. Adding another coat or two will produce a soft luster.

In some cases, a clear finish is best. After cleaning the piece, use a sponge applicator or a natural-bristle paintbrush to apply a clear acrylic finish. Add three coats, allowing plenty of drying time in between.

CLEANING FINISHED WOOD

The most important ingredient for cleaning wood is common sense. Cleaning a rustic piece that's been in a barn for 30 years is simple. A fine piece that has a shellacked or lacquered finish requires a different approach.

Let's start with the rustics. This is a look I love: Old and cruddy is my thing, but I don't want to bring dirt into my house, and don't imagine you do, either. In good weather, start outside with a hose, a soft scrub brush, and some mild soap and water. If that's not possible, work at a utility sink or in a large bucket.

When the weather permits, let the piece dry outdoors in the sun, to give it a chance to air out and lose any musty odor it might have. If a musty odor persists, wash the piece again with a weak bleach and water solution. Rinse the wood thoroughly with a vinegar solution to neutralize the bleach and then with water to remove any residue. Let the piece dry overnight.

Apply a light coat of beeswax and buff it with a clean, soft, lint-free cloth; add two more coats. To maintain this finish, wax the piece whenever the wood looks dry or when a drop of water won't bead up on the surface.

Shellacked or lacquered finishes require more careful handling. Wash these pieces with a soft cloth and a weak vinegar and water solution. On stubborn spots you can use an old, soft toothbrush if necessary.

REPAIRING SURFACE FLAWS

Most of the time, it's best to leave minor imperfections exactly as they are—they provide character. But there are some situations where it makes sense to repair minor surface flaws, and it's usually fairly easy to do.

Shallow dents can be raised with water or steam. Start by applying a few drops of distilled water into the dent; let the water soak in. In most cases, the dented wood will swell back to its original shape. If not, place a wet rag directly over the dent; touch the rag with the tip of a hot iron. The resulting steam often causes the wood to swell back into shape. If that fails, fill the dent with wood putty.

Minor scratches or dents can be filled with wood putty. To get rid of debris that could keep the putty from bonding, clean out the damaged area with a pointed scraper, such as a modeling tool. If the flaw is very shallow, make it a little deeper. Next, use a putty knife to fill the damaged area with stainable wood putty. Scrape away the excess, leaving the putty just slightly above the surface of the wood. When the putty is dry, sand the area until the putty is level with the wood surface. To blend the repair into the area, color the putty with stain or a touch-up marker that matches the color of the wood.

Water damage or contact with metal sometimes creates black stains on wood. These stains can be removed with a mixture of oxalic acid crystals and distilled water. Paint the solution onto the stain and let it soak in. Rinse and repeat as necessary.

Chlorine bleach will remove many spot stains. Working in an area with good ventilation, brush undiluted bleach onto the stain and wait 20 minutes. To help activate the bleach, set the workpiece out in direct sunlight. Rinse the bleach with water and reapply as necessary. As soon as you're finished, neutralize the bleach: Wipe white vinegar onto the area and then rinse it immediately with water.

RE-GLUING VENEERS

Making basic veneer repairs, such as re-gluing loose or blistered veneer, is a fairly simple job. More complicated repairs involving patching should be left to professionals.

Before deciding to re-glue loose veneer, try using heat to renew the bond. Cover the loosened veneer with a damp cloth; press the cloth with a household iron set on low. Keep the iron moving—don't leave it in place for more than a few seconds. Wait for the veneer glue to liquefy, then remove the iron and the cloth. Before the glue rehardens, roll the area with a seam roller. Set a weight such as a heavy book on the area as it cools.

If ironing doesn't work, re-glue the loose spots. Use a putty or palette knife to lift the veneer so you can clean below it with a brush. Veneer is fragile—be careful not to tear it. If there's glue on the surface, scrub it with a cotton swab dipped in hot vinegar. Next, use a cotton swab or a glue injector to squeeze glue under the veneer. Cover the area with wax paper and a clamping block and clamp the area until the glue dries. Remove the clamp and carefully scrape away any excess glue with a chisel.

Missing sections of veneer are difficult to repair. If you still have the missing piece and it's intact, it can be re-glued in the way described above. If you don't have the pieces, get professional help. Cutting and gluing down new veneer patches is a job that requires finesse and experience.

Blistered veneer can be repaired in much the same way as loose veneer. Start by using a craft knife to slice the blister along the grain. Use a small brush to clean out any debris, then slip a thin spacer under the veneer. Inject carpenter's glue into the area, roll the blister with a seam roller, and cover the area with wax paper. Clamp or weight the loose veneer down until the glue dries. If the veneer overlaps at the seam, slice away the excess, using a craft knife and a straightedge.

REPAIRING JOINTS & SPLITS

Loose joints and split parts, common structural problems, usually can be corrected by gluing and reinforcing the joints.

Use wood sweller to tighten loose joints on parts that don't support much weight, such as interior spindles on a chair. Just squirt the wood sweller into the joint and let it sit—the wood in the joint will swell and tighten.

To repair a split spindle, start by cleaning debris and splinters from the pieces so the mating surfaces fit tightly. Apply glue to the mating surfaces, wrap the spindle with wax paper, then press the parts together. Slip hose clamps over the repair, spaced every 3 to 4" (7 to 10 cm); tighten the clamps. Let the glue dry, remove the clamps and paper, and scrape away the excess glue with a chisel.

Structural joints that need to support weight can be repaired with two-part epoxy. Drill at least two $\frac{3}{16}$"-diameter (5 mm) holes per joint. Using a self-mixing injector, deliver two-part epoxy glue into each hole. The epoxy will harden into "nails" that will reinforce the joints.

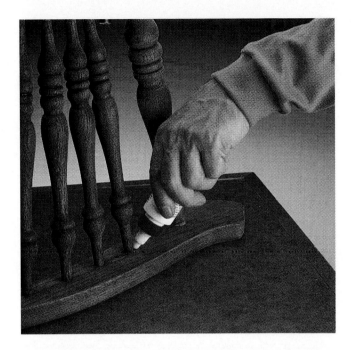

PATCHING DAMAGED WOOD

We use doors in several projects throughout the book, and although interesting doors are easy to find, they're sometimes damaged by rot—especially screen doors, which are exposed to the elements. You may also find this kind of damage in other pieces you'd like to use. It can be remedied with epoxy wood filler, which can be molded and shaped easily, and readily accepts paint or stain.

Start by removing the damaged wood with a chisel or utility knife. (Wear eye protection while chiseling wood.) Build simple wood forms as needed to establish boundaries for the repair. Coat the forms with wax or oil so the filler won't stick to them.

Mix and apply the wood filler, according to package instructions. Use a putty knife or trowel to shape the repair area to match the existing contours. Let the filler harden completely.

Remove the forms and lightly sand the hardened filler. Use a light hand—oversanding closes the filler's pores and makes it difficult to stain. Paint or stain the wood to match the existing finish.

CLEANING METAL, LEATHER & CANVAS

As copper, brass, and bronze age, they develop a patina, called *verdigris*, in various shades of green, blue, and brown. Iron, tin, and other metals develop a layer of oxidation known as rust. Both verdigris and rust add an interesting range of colors and textures to an old piece.

To remove rust from metal, use fine steel wool and lubricant oil, such as WD-40®. Scour carefully, working in circles. When you're finished, wipe the area with mineral spirits to remove the oil residue. Let the area dry, then wipe it again with a clean cloth.

To clean and preserve a surface covered with rust or verdigris, wash the piece with a 1:1 vinegar and water solution and let it dry.

In either case, apply a light coat of clear acrylic sealer and let that dry. Add three or four coats of sealer, letting it dry between coats. If you want to preserve the current level of oxidation on an iron piece, use a rust-inhibiting sealer.

Note: Sealing a weathered surface may darken the patina's color somewhat.

Use Liquid Steel filler to patch any holes or tears in tin. Badly damaged areas can be replaced: Cut away the old tin, using tin snips, and nail on new pieces. Use Liquid Steel filler to bridge the ridge between the old tin and the patch. If necessary, touch up the area with rust-inhibiting metal primer and enamel paint.

Use saddle soap and a soft rag to clean leather. Let the leather dry, then polish it with a leather dressing, such as mink oil. Use all-purpose cement to re-glue any tears.

Scrub canvas gently, using a brush and mild soap. Re-glue any loose areas, using wood glue diluted with an equal amount of water.

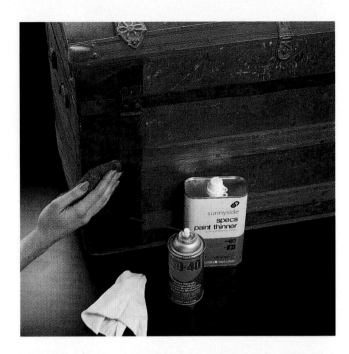

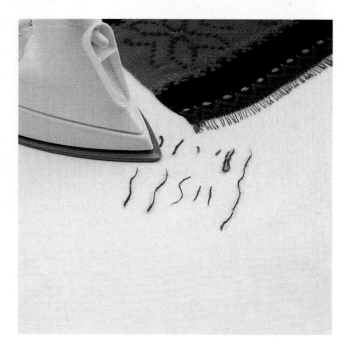

CLEANING & RESTORING LINENS

In some ways, textiles carry their stories more than other old pieces. Stains, wear, and mending or signs of alterations give us clues about the people who owned and used these things. Gentle cleaning is important—it protects fibers and prevents deterioration—but it's not always necessary or even a good idea to remove every trace of the history.

When shopping for old textiles, look for pieces in good condition. If you're planning to cut apart a piece to use the fabric in a decorating project, you may be able to work around stains, holes, or weak areas. Remember that it may not be possible to remove stains, and in the process of trying, you may even cause the fabric to disintegrate further.

Old silks are likely to be weighted with metallic salts, lead, or arsenic; handling them can be hazardous. Old silk is extremely fragile and when torn, it releases harmful fibers.

Fabric becomes even more fragile when wet. Before cleaning old garments and quilts, repair any open seams and reinforce areas around holes or weak spots. It's a good idea to stitch around the outer edges of unfinished pieces, such as needlepoint canvases, quilt tops, or individual quilt blocks, but it isn't necessary to stitch around the selvages of tapestries.

Test the stability of the dyes before washing a textile. Remove yarns of each color or a small piece of fabric from a seam allowance or edge. Lay the pieces on white cotton and press them with a warm steam iron; let them dry for 10 minutes. If dye bleeds onto the white fabric, dry clean the textile instead of washing it.

If it's necessary to dry clean a fragile textile, take it to a dry cleaner who uses the flat dry-cleaning method, which creates less abrasion than the tumble method.

Wash a piece of fiberglass screening and bind the edges with tape. Place the screening in the bottom of a laundry sink or bathtub. Fill the tub with lukewarm or cool water and a small amount of a gentle soap.

Put especially fragile items in a pillowcase or mesh bag before washing them; lay the textile in soapy water and press against it with the palm of your hand rather than agitating or wringing it. For heavily soiled items, change the washing solution often. Rinse several times; make sure you remove all traces of soap residue. Use distilled water for the final rinse.

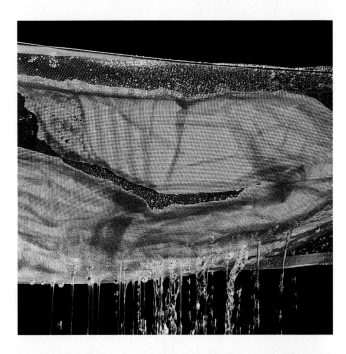

Lift the screening from the bottom of the tub, bringing the fabric along with it. Roll the laundered textile in a white towel to remove the excess moisture; lay the piece flat and pat it into its original shape. Let the fabric air dry only until it's slightly damp. (Directing a fan toward it speeds up the process.)

Iron the piece while the fabric's still damp—when fabric dries completely, it temporarily loses its natural moisture and becomes brittle. And when you iron vintage linens, don't use steam or starch. Steam can bring stains to the surface, and starch can attract pests over time.

To clean vintage lace or doilies, rub a thick paste of salt and white vinegar into spots, using a toothbrush. Next, soak the pieces for an hour or so in a 3:1 solution of water and vinegar. Rinse thoroughly until clean.

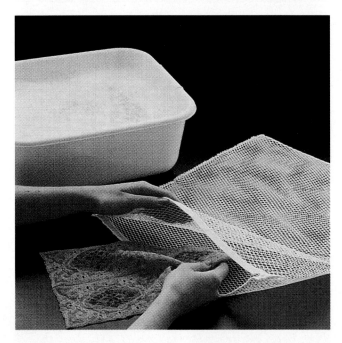

Drying white linens in the sun helps naturally bleach and brighten them.

To avoid mildew, make sure linens are clean before you put them away; keep them in dry, well-ventilated cabinets or closets. Don't store vintage linens in plastic bags—air flow helps the fibers breathe. Lining the shelves or drawers helps reduce exposure to wood fumes, which can cause premature yellowing.

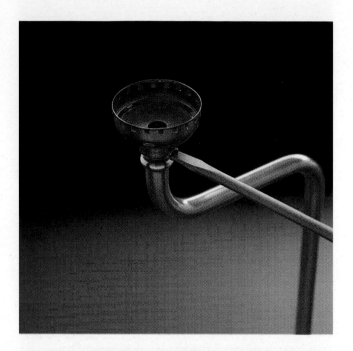

WIRING LAMPS

The first time I made a lamp, I was stunned at how easy it was to do the wiring. I guess it seemed mysterious and complicated because I had no idea how few steps it really takes. Basically, all you have to do is thread the lamp cord through the base and up to the socket, and then connect two wires. Very simple—it will probably take less than half an hour to do the whole thing, even the first time. The next time, it will take just a matter of minutes.

Thread the lamp cord through the base and up through the lamp pipe. (Most lamp cords are pre-split and the ends are stripped in preparation for wiring. If yours isn't, use a utility knife to split the first 2" [5 cm] of the end of the cord, along the midline of the insulation. Strip about ½ to ¾" [12 to 19 mm] of insulation from the ends of the wires.)

Tie an underwriter's knot by forming an overhand loop with one wire and an underhand loop with the remaining wire; insert each wire end through the loop of the other wire.

Loosen the terminal screws on the socket. Look carefully at the insulation on the wires—the insulation on one wire will be rounded and on the other wire it will be ribbed or will have a fine line on it. Loop the wire on the rounded side around the socket's brass screw and tighten the screw. Loop the wire on the ribbed side around the socket's silver screw and tighten the screw.

Adjust the underwriter's knot to fit within the base of the socket cap, then position the socket into the socket cap. Slide the insulating sleeve and outer shell over the socket so the terminal screws are fully covered and any slots are correctly aligned. Test the lamp; when you're sure it works, press the socket assembly down into the socket cap until the socket locks into place.

*F*URNISHINGS

Things change. People change. A room that suited you one year may not be quite right the next. One of the great things about a flea-market-style home is that it's always evolving, right along with your interests and tastes. Since furnishings form the foundation of a room's personality, adding or replacing a piece or two lets you refresh it without starting over from scratch.

To be comfortable, a room needs plenty of resting places—sofas, chairs, beds, benches—where you can sit and think, or read, or talk with family and friends. Ottomans are great when you want to put your feet up, but they also can be used as seating or even serving space when you're entertaining. As you can tell from the mosaic chair and the topiary chair projects in this chapter, there are many nontraditional ways to use seating pieces, if you look at them creatively.

Flea markets typically offer a wide variety of pieces that provide storage—chests, armoires, Hoosier cabinets, trunks, and so forth. It's important to have both open and enclosed storage in every room. For example, I like to keep quilts and other linens in the open (but out of direct sunlight) because they add color and texture. I also need lots of bookshelves and display pieces because every room in my home contains books, family photographs, and other reminders of the people I love. On the other hand, we all need storage pieces with doors that can be closed over the clutter that's perpetually waiting for attention.

It's always a good idea to keep an eye out for great tables or things that could be used for tables. In this chapter we show you how to make a hallway table/shelf out of an old corbel, and a coffee table out of some old porch balusters, but who knows what might catch your eye and send your imagination racing?

SURPRISE

Using furnishings and materials in unexpected ways is a big part of the fun of flea market style. For instance, there are many ways to use an old fireplace surround and mantle, even in rooms that don't have fireplaces. Combined with a trompe l'oeil scene and a hand-hooked hearth rug, the mantle and surround shown in the photo above create a cozy nook for reading, and anchor a display of framed art and Hummel figurines.

It may not be traditional, but there's no reason you shouldn't put furniture in a bathroom if you have the space. In the spacious bathroom shown at left, a dresser offers linen storage; a desk and chair, which replace an ordinary vanity, create a comfortable, convenient place to do hair and make-up.

BALANCE

As you decide where and how to use your flea market treasures, think of each room's furnishings as the raw materials of a composition you're creating. Try to balance the shapes, sizes, colors, and textures. In the room shown above, the substantial armchair and storage/display piece contrast with the high legs of the console and plant stand as well as the airy shape and texture of the ottoman. I like the way the silhouette of the amaryllis in the framed art is echoed by the shape and position of the candlestick lamp and by the detail on the doors of the storage unit.

In the room at right, the open lines of the side chair and stool balance the weight of the armchair and sideboard. The texture of the shutters pairs nicely with that of the sideboard doors; the mixture of patterns in the fabrics and rug plays well against neutral walls and white accents. Even among the accessories, intricate shapes mingle with simple ones; pedestals are used to position interesting elements at staggered heights, in contrast to the predominately parallel lines, throughout the room.

RAW MATERIALS

Once you've learned to recognize unique ways to use vintage pieces, stretch the boundaries of your imagination even further. To the practiced eye, discarded porch railings, salvaged window sashes or doors—even tree branches and chicken wire—can become the raw materials from which to create the furnishings that will set your home apart as special and unique.

Someone fashioned tree branches into a fanciful daybed for the sitting room shown at right. Surrounded by collections of eclectic accessories, it looks right at home.

The chicken wire vase also is evidence of some serious imagination at work, and it wouldn't be hard to duplicate. Just use a pair of tin snips to cut the chicken wire, and then shape it into a cylinder, overlapping the edges by about 1" (2.5 cm). Crimp the lower edges of the cylinder toward the center to form the bottom of the "vase," then use fine-gauge wire to join the layers of chicken wire. To avoid being scratched while arranging flowers, you might want to crimp the wire at the top edges of the cylinder, too. Although these are dried flowers, you could easily use fresh ones—simply set a clear glass vase in the center and then camouflage it with carefully arranged stones or shells or pieces of handmade paper.

Friends often laugh over the stuff I find valuable. Inevitably, when I'm scavenging, someone will question why in the world I would want such a thing. Most of the time, I honestly don't know what will become of the oddities I find; I'm just sure they need to come home with me.

If I let a piece sit within plain sight for a few weeks, chances are that an idea will materialize. When people ask about a strange object sitting around my home or office, I usually explain that I'm waiting for it to tell me what it wants to be.

This brings up a good point: While it's good to have a backlog of materials on hand, be careful not to get carried away. If the stockpile grows to the point that you no longer remember what you have, it's just taking up space. If you haven't used something in a couple of years, discard it or give it to a friend.

BREAKING THEM IN

Tim's mother once came in from hanging out the wash to find three-year-old Tim and his four-year-old sister, Joy, hurling her best china at the dining room buffet. They were having a great time, laughing at the clatter they were making as the dishes broke and the buffet rocked. Tim's folks still have that scarred buffet, and Tim and Joy still hear its tale at family gatherings.

No matter how your dishes get broken, you can use them in a simple mosaic that transforms an ordinary ice cream parlor chair into something special.

1. *Loosen the bolts holding the chair bottom; remove the plywood and upholstery materials. Trace the outline of the chair frame onto the plywood.*

2. *If you're trying to preserve a center medallion, put masking tape across the back of the plate. Place the plate in a paper bag and tap it with a rubber mallet. Use tile nippers to refine the pieces. Glue the pieces to the plywood, within the outline of the frame.*

3. *Replace the plywood and tighten the bolts. Apply grout to the mosaic. Use a damp sponge to clean away the excess grout. Rinse the sponge frequently and keep wiping until all the grit has been removed. Several hours later, remove the grout film by polishing the mosaic with a dry cloth.*

MATERIALS:

ICE CREAM PARLOR CHAIR • CHINA PLATES • SILICONE GLUE • GROUT

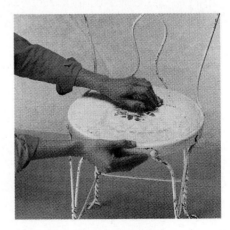

POTTING IT TOGETHER

Salvaged lumber has a romance about it—the wood itself holds memories and stories. When I was a kid, my dad rescued some walnut boards from my great-grandpa's barn. We hauled those boards, tied to the top of a '59 Ford, from south-central Iowa to California. Just before the state line, Dad rigged a way to hide them under the car so we could get them through California's border patrol—the only illegal thing I ever saw my father do. It was worth the effort: Each piece Dad built from that lumber is a treasure.

If you have or can find salvaged lumber to go with the old window sash for this potting bench, it will add another dimension to the project. If not, you could "weather" cedar lumber to achieve nearly the same effect. All you need to do is dissolve baking soda in hot water, about 1 part baking soda to 5 parts water. Spray the solution onto the boards and set them in bright sunlight—they'll turn a lovely shade of gray.

MATERIALS:

SALVAGED WINDOW SASH • 1½" (38 MM) WOOD SCREWS • 1¼" (31 MM) WOOD SCREWS • ½" (12 MM) WOOD SCREWS • 2" (5 CM) WOOD SCREWS • ½" (12 MM) PLYWOOD • ANGLE IRON • PLANTING BASIN • 2 × 4 (5 × 10 CM) LUMBER • 1 × 4 (2.5 × 10 CM) LUMBER • 1 × 2 (2.5 × 5 CM) LUMBER • 1 × 6 (2.5 × 15 CM) LUMBER

◆1 Measure the window sash. Lay out the two 2 × 4 (5 × 10 cm) back legs and determine where to position the braces, based on the dimensions of the sash. Drill pilot holes and attach both 1 × 4 (2.5 × 10 cm) horizontal braces and then the 1 × 2 (2.5 × 5 cm) vertical braces, using 1½" (38 mm) wood screws. Use angle iron and ½" (12 mm) wood screws to attach the 1 × 6 (2.5 × 15 cm) ledge, flush with the back of the lower horizontal brace. On the back face of the back legs, add the 1 × 4 (2.5 × 10 cm) lower horizontal brace, driving the screws from the front of the brace.

◆2 Assemble the 2 × 4 (5 × 10 cm) front legs and 1 × 4 (2.5 × 10 cm) upper and lower side braces, using 2" (5 cm) wood screws. Attach these assemblies to the back frame, securing the upper side braces to the outside edge of the back legs with 2" (5 cm) wood screws.

◆3 Attach the upper front brace and then add the mid-table brace. Attach the lower front brace.

◆4 Lay the 1 × 6 (2.5 × 15 cm) decking on the lower shelf, securing each piece with pairs of screws driven into each lower side brace. Next, lay the 1 × 6 (2.5 × 15 cm) decking on the tabletop, driving pairs of screws into each upper side brace as well as the mid-table brace. Measure the planting basin; cut a square piece of ½" (12 mm) plywood, 4" (10 cm) larger than the circumference of the basin. Trace the basin onto the plywood, and use a jig saw to cut out the hole. Position this plywood brace to indicate the hole for the planting basin, and trace the cutout onto the decking. From below, attach the plywood to the underside of the decking, driving two 1¼" (31 mm) wood screws through the brace and into each decking board. Use a jig saw to cut along the marked lines to make the hole in the decking for the planting basin.

◆5 Set the window into position and secure it to the horizontal braces, using 2" (5 cm) wood screws.

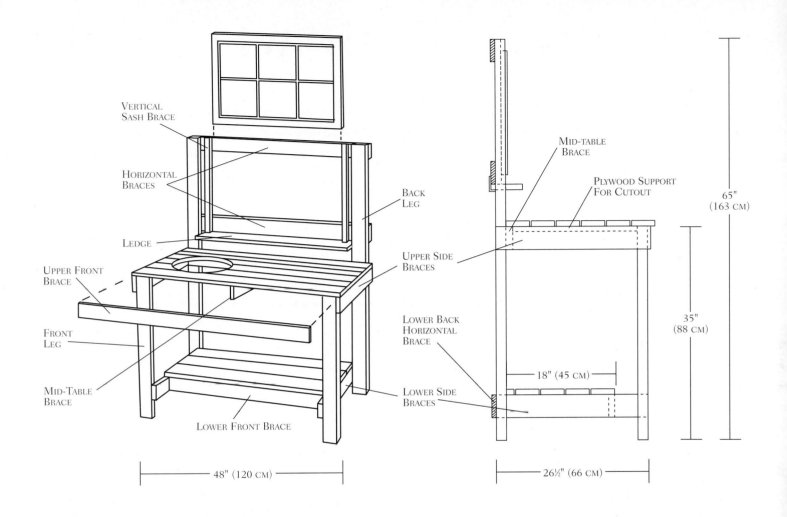

VERTICAL SASH BRACE

HORIZONTAL BRACES

LEDGE

UPPER FRONT BRACE

FRONT LEG

MID-TABLE BRACE

LOWER FRONT BRACE

BACK LEG

UPPER SIDE BRACES

LOWER BACK HORIZONTAL BRACE

LOWER SIDE BRACES

MID-TABLE BRACE

PLYWOOD SUPPORT FOR CUTOUT

65" (163 CM)

35" (88 CM)

18" (45 CM)

48" (120 CM)

26½" (66 CM)

HOLDING UP WELL

Too bulky to grace a counter or a tabletop, this dough bowl acted as a catch-all in my sewing room for several years before I hit on the idea of building a stand for it. Now it holds seasonal displays or fresh flowers or potted ferns, depending on the time of year and my mood. It would also make a nice place to keep hats and mittens.

If you have a similar piece, you may have the same problem. If you don't have one but like the looks of this project, you should be able to find a dough bowl pretty easily—you often see them at flea markets and sales.

◆1 *Measure the circumference of your dough bowl, approximately 3"*
(7.5 cm) from the top. Cut and dry-fit ½" (12 mm) copper pipe and
fittings to form a frame and legs, as indicated in the drawing below. You'll
have to adjust the dimensions, but the general design should work for most
dough bowls of this type. When you have all the pieces cut and fit properly,
clean the pipe and solder the joints, working from the bottom up.

◆2 *Wrap wire around the horizontal brace between a pair of legs and*
extend it to the diagonally opposite pair of legs; wrap the wire around the
brace. Repeat with the opposite pair of legs. Solder each wrapped section.
Wrap the intersection of the wires and solder it as well.

MATERIALS:
WOODEN DOUGH BOWL • ½" (12 MM) COPPER PIPE • ½" (12 MM) COPPER TEES AND ELBOWS
• 8-GAUGE (4MM) COPPER WIRE • ½" (12 MM) COPPER END CAPS (8) • FLUX • SOLDER

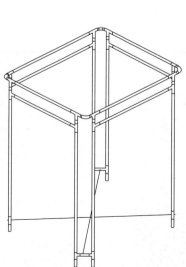

REINVENTION

It's a special pleasure to use furnishings that are both beautiful and functional. With little or no alteration, the former mail-sorting cubby in the photo at left became a wine rack. Supporting a collection of farm memorabilia above and cradling matching wicker trunks below, it contributes a homey ambience to the room while providing much needed storage for a growing wine collection. This piece is perfect for its place—the geometric arrangement of the cubbies even repeats the pattern of the floor tiles.

Some people seem to think that recycling is an invention of the 20th century. Nothing could be further from the truth. Generations ago, for example, clothing was handed down and worn until it was threadbare, then the buttons were cut off and the fabric saved for rugs or quilts. One of my mother's most cherished possessions is a quilt made from the remnants of clothing she or her siblings had worn—there are even a few precious bits from my grandma's old aprons. Now that's recycling!

In the photo at right above, gorgeous fabric, antique buttons, salvaged millwork, and hardware rescued from an old dresser team up to produce a unique window treatment. The idea here, like the window treatment on pages 58 and 59, is relatively simple and entirely possible for anyone to accomplish, but both depend on having access to the right materials.

It's a good idea to get into the habit of saving the hardware from anything you discard. If you're planning to sell a piece or donate it to charity, first exchange the original hardware with inexpensive but serviceable replacements. Of course, if you're selling the piece you should be honest with the buyer and price the piece accordingly.

Once you get interested in adapting and refurbishing flea market treasures, you may find yourself lingering over boxes of mismatched hardware at flea markets or searching through the rubble at architectural salvage places. You never know when or how that hardware will come in handy, but you can be sure that, in time, it will.

The next step in having the materials you need when you want them is storing them in a way that makes them easy to find. If possible, set up a workshop, complete with storage bins that let you keep like with like—all your door knobs in one bin and hinges in another, for example. If that's not realistic, try resealable plastic bags stored in sturdy, stackable, well-labeled cardboard or clear plastic boxes.

EXOTICS

The claw-foot tub above is being used outdoors as a planter, but there's no reason you couldn't do the same thing indoors, if you have the space. You might, however, want to plug the drainage hole so that water doesn't find its way to the floor when you water the plants. With a few minor adaptations, you could also transform an old tub into a water garden.

An element that appears to be foreign or out of context is sometimes known as an *exotic*. In the great room at right, the rustic table and twig footstool appear exotic in contrast with the room's other sleeker, more polished furnishings. Don't be afraid to include unique pieces in your rooms. Like the exception that proves the rule, their very contrast can pull a room together, giving it warmth and personality.

Remember the cardinal rule of flea market style: If you absolutely love it, it works.

COMMON THREADS

The trick to combining a wide variety of elements is to find the relationship between them and then put them together in ways that emphasize what they have in common. The alcove beside the stairs at right illustrates this idea perfectly. The simple lines of the bookcases and the writing table blend well, forming the basis for a reading nook. The bench, lamp, and other accessories invite you to linger there in comfort. Their common purpose unites the various pieces and produces a feeling of harmony among them, despite their differences.

Color unites the elements of the setting in the photo above. The vivid tones of the stained-glass window are picked up by the colors of the window trim, table, and rug. In the type of strong light you see streaming through the window, brilliant colors are effective. The stronger the light, the more intense a color needs to be to create an impression. Subtle colors such as pastels, which glow in dim light, would look washed out here.

WARM WELCOME

Years ago—long before it became trendy—I came across the term *feng shui* in a novel and became interested in the art and science of effective room arrangements. Although some current books and magazines make it sound like New Age nonsense, at its essence, feng shui is based on sensible, practical issues.

One of its principles is to welcome energy into your home and then to direct it positively. This simple combination of a corbel and a plywood shelf produces a pleasing way to invite energy into your home.

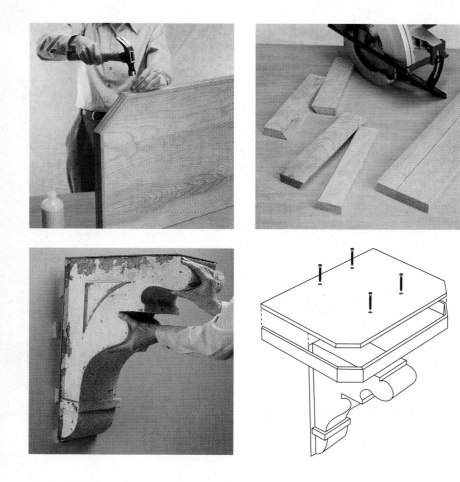

1 Cut a piece of ¾" (19 mm) plywood for the top. (The dimensions will depend on the size of the corbel you're using. We made ours 32 × 20" [80 × 50 cm]). Trim the edges of the corners as shown. Cut ogee molding to fit the top, mitering the corners. Glue and tack molding along the front and sides of the tabletop. Paint or finish the top to match or complement your corbel.

2 Mark a line down the 1 × 4 (2.5 × 10 cm), 1⅜" (34 mm) from the long edge. Set the bevel on a circular saw to 45° and cut along the marked line. Reset the bevel on the circular saw to 90° and cut two pairs of mating cleats to match the width of your corbel. Use 2" (5 cm) screws to attach two cleats to the back of the corbel—one near the top and the other near the lower edge.

3 Hold the corbel in place and mark the locations for the mating cleats. Screw the cleats to the wall. Be sure you hit a stud or use hollow wall anchors to support the weight.

4 Set the tabletop in place; drill two counterbored pilot holes through it and down into the corbel. Secure the top to the corbel with 2" (5 cm) screws. Fill the holes and touch up the paint.

MATERIALS:

CORBEL • ¾" (19 MM) AB INTERIOR PLYWOOD • OGEE MOLDING • WOOD GLUE
• 4D FINISH NAILS • 2" (5 CM) WOOD SCREWS • PAINT OR STAIN • PINE 1 × 4 (2.5 × 10 CM)

STAYING IN THE VIEW

To bring the outdoors into a room, think of the windows as art to be framed—it's surprising how much more compelling a view becomes when you surround it with a unique window treatment.

Note: for windows wider than 40" (1 m), support the pipe with three doorknobs.

1 *Loosen the set screw and remove the stem from each knob. Use two-part epoxy to glue a knob into each escutcheon.*

2 *Locate the studs near the outside edges of the window. Hold the escutcheons in position, mark and drill pilot holes, and use 2" (5 cm) brass screws to hang them. If there are no studs in suitable locations, use wall anchors to support the weight.*

3 *Cut two pieces of silk cord, about 30" (75 cm) long. Tie a knot 2" (5 cm) above the bottom of each cord; fray the cord below the knot. String beads onto the cord, stacking them to about 4½" (11 cm). Loop the cord and hold the loop in place with several twists of 16-gauge (1.5 mm) copper wire. Stack another inch or two (2 to 5 cm) of beads and knot the cord again. Cut a piece of copper pipe about 16" (40 cm) longer than the window's width. Glue end caps to the pipe, then set it on top of the doorknobs. Arrange your fabric or drapes over the pipe and allow it to hang down the sides of the window. Tie the beaded cord to the pipe, between the doorknob and the window trim.*

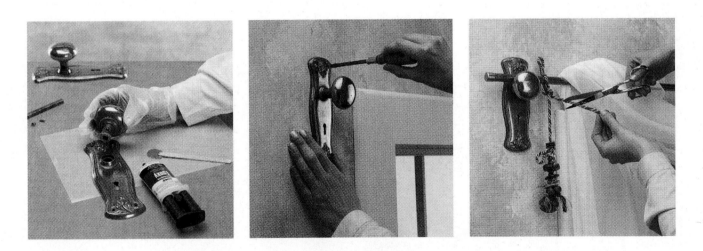

MATERIALS:

ANTIQUE DOORKNOBS AND ESCUTCHEONS (2 EACH) • TWO-PART EPOXY • 2" (5 CM) BRASS SCREWS (4)
• 16-GAUGE (1.5 MM) COPPER WIRE • ½" (12 MM) COPPER PIPE • ½" (12 MM) COPPER END CAPS (2)
• BRASS FINIALS (OPTIONAL) • SATIN CORD (2 YARDS [1.8 M]) • BEADS

A LEG TO STAND ON

Spending a week with my mother's parents in Iowa was the highlight of my childhood summers. One of my favorite parts was sitting on the front porch. It was there that we snapped beans for supper, drank ice tea, and caught whatever breeze came along on a stifling summer afternoon. In the evenings, Grandma and Grandpa sat in metal clamshell chairs to watch my cousins and me capture fireflies in mayonnaise jars.

As decks became more popular, porches literally took a back seat, but these days they're making a comeback as many of us look for ways to reconnect with one another. Meantime, flea markets and architectural salvage places frequently offer porch railings.

Looking at a discarded section of railing one day, I realized that the balusters were a perfect size to be made into table legs. It's surprisingly easy, and even if you've never snapped a bean in your life, you might appreciate the gracious atmosphere the table provides.

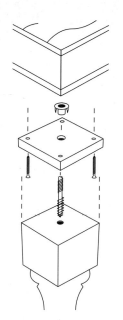

1. Cut a plywood tabletop in proportion to suit the balusters (ours is 42 × 20" [105 × 50 cm]); cut trim molding to fit, mitering the ends. Paint or finish the top and molding to match or complement the balusters. Attach the molding to the tabletop, using glue and finish nails. Cut four 4½ × 4½" (11 × 11 cm) blocks of ½" (12 mm) birch, and drill a ⁵⁄₁₆" (8 mm) hole through the center of each. Install a T-nut in each block.

2. Attach a block 1" (2.5 cm) from the corner on each side; secure the blocks with glue and ¾" (19 mm) wood screws.

3. Gang the balusters and compare them. Plane or sand them as necessary until the ends are flush with one another. At the top of each baluster, drill a ⅛" (3 mm) pilot hole and install a furniture bolt. Install the baluster legs by screwing the bolts into the T-nuts. If necessary, add leveling feet to the bottoms of the balusters.

MATERIALS:

PORCH BALUSTERS (4) • ¾" (19 MM) BIRCH PLYWOOD • OGEE MOLDING • WOOD GLUE • 4D FINISH NAILS • SCRAP OF ½" (12 MM) BIRCH • ¾" (19 MM) WOOD SCREWS (4) • T-NUTS (4) • FURNITURE BOLTS (4)

THEME

Some of my favorite flea market finds are storage pieces. I brought home the cabinet shown on pages 72 and 73, tied to the roof of my car like a hunting trophy. Which, I guess, it really was. Now it proudly sits in my sewing room, holding quilt tops waiting to be finished, out-of-season linens, and toys my children have outgrown. In my family room, a stack of carpenter's tool chests doubles as an end table, and a seaman's chest sits nearby, acting as a coffeetable.

When we live with our collections, they become more than just more stuff. And collections of trunks or suitcases or baskets have a unique advantage: They can be used to store other stuff. The owner of the suitcase collection in the photo at left knows this secret—the room's central theme seems to be storage. And it works—the effect is attractive, practical, and interesting.

The kitchen shown above features a collection of food storage items. Imagine the picnics those baskets have held and the ones yet to be produced from that beautiful pantry. Someone who owns canisters like that just has to be a good cook.

TRANSFORMATION

Finding inspired ways to use found objects is the essence of flea market style. In the bathroom at right, an old table has been adapted into a stylish vanity. It fits the style of the room beautifully and seems perfect for its place. The details on the legs are shown to great advantage, and the tabletop gracefully accommodates a sink and bath accessories.

In some cases, finding a treasure is only half the fun—the other half is adapting the piece to a practical purpose. You do need to think carefully before you make any changes to a flea market find. If there's any chance you're about to reduce or destroy the value of an antique or rare primitive piece, stop in your tracks. Consult an expert before doing anything you might regret.

Most of the time, you won't have to worry about making that kind of mistake. The price you paid for the piece will guide you, and so will its condition. Let's say, for example, you found a table like this one, in great shape except for a ruined top. Clearly, the top must be refinished or replaced anyway, so the decision to alter it isn't something to agonize over. From there, it's not much of a leap to cutting an opening for the sink and drilling holes for the faucet—all you need are the right tools and a steady hand.

If you don't have much experience with power tools or do-it-yourself projects, do some research before beginning. Don't be intimidated; you can learn to do just about anything required to adapt a piece to your purposes. Start at a bookstore or library. There are many good books available to help you learn to finish or refinish wood, produce a variety of painted finishes, or do a broad range of typical repairs. Most of these projects won't require anything beyond a few tools, a little patience, and a good dose of common sense. (My mother says that the least common thing in the world is common sense. While that may be true, we can all develop some if we apply ourselves.)

If you don't have the time or any interest in doing these projects yourself, develop a network of people who can help. There are few people more useful to know than a good carpenter; a skilled woodworker would be helpful, too. While the hourly rates commanded by these craftspeople might seem steep, their knowledge and abilities are worth the expense.

FINISHES

Color provides a central theme for the room shown above: Black and white is repeated throughout the painted furniture, fabrics, and accessories. Small splashes of pink and red provide contrast and soften the palette to suit the room's lively tone. If you want to create a room in this type of style, first decide on your theme, then shop for pieces that can be worked into your overall plan. For example, the turned spindles on the chair gave this artist the opportunity to add blocks of black here and there, the drop-leaf table in the background provided a broad vertical surface on which to repeat the rose motif from the cabinet, and the round table practically begged to be skirted.

Inexpensive or reproduction pieces can be enhanced with an imaginative application of paint, but with fine old pieces or primitives, more often than not you'll want to keep the character added by worn finishes or multiple layers of paint. With a finish such as the one on the hutch in the photo at right, a careful scrubbing with mild soap and warm water is all that's necessary, or even wise.

FLOOR TO CEILING

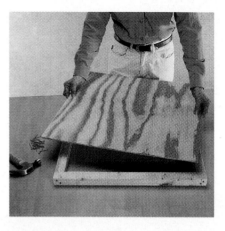

Tin ceiling tiles were originally developed as an economical alternative to elaborate European carved plasterwork. They were popular throughout North America from the mid-nineteenth century to the early twentieth, and as buildings and homes from that era have been torn down or remodeled, many of the tiles have been salvaged.

Whether painted, lacquered, or plated, these embossed panels are beautiful. They're also easy to work with and relatively inexpensive. We used a couple of panels to convert a simple wooden box into a striking planter.

1 Assemble 2 × 2 (5 × 5 cm) frames as shown in the illustration. Secure plywood to each frame, using glue and wood screws.

2 Join the frames into a box, and then add plywood to the bottom.

3 Run several beads of construction adhesive across the backs of the ceiling tiles, and then clamp them in place. Cut the 1 × 3s (2.5 × 7.5 cm) and corner trim; paint the 1 × 3s (2.5 × 7.5 cm), the corner trim, and the 2 × 2 (5 × 5 cm) at the top of each frame to match or complement your ceiling tiles. Drill pilot holes and nail the 1 × 3s (2.5 × 7.5 cm) to the bottom of the planter; add the corner trim in the same way.

MATERIALS:

TIN CEILING TILE • 2 × 2s (5 × 5 CM) • ¼" (6 MM) PLYWOOD
• 1 × 3s (2.5 × 7.5 CM) • CONSTRUCTION ADHESIVE • WOOD GLUE
• 2½" (6 CM) WOOD SCREWS • PAINT OR STAIN • CORNER TRIM

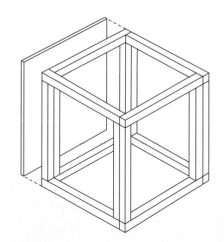

Thanks for the Memories

Tim's a packrat. He came by it naturally—his grandfather saved every receipt he ever received. They filled a five-drawer file. Tim himself keeps an enormous memory album of ticket stubs, expired driver's licenses, student IDs, even one gum wrapper. (I'm dying to know the story of that gum wrapper, but when I ask, Tim just smiles.)

Although most of us don't go to those extremes, we do like to keep mementos—invitations, cards, tickets, photos. This ribbon board provides attractive display space for just those sorts of things.

1 *Remove the mirror from its mirror frame. Clean, sand, and paint the frame. Measure the opening and cut a piece of ⅜" (9 mm) plywood to fit.*

2 *Cut quilt batting 2" (5 cm) larger than the plywood; cut fabric 3" (7.5 cm) larger. Layer the fabric (right side down), the batting, and the plywood. Wrap the batting and fabric around the plywood, keeping the grain straight and the fabric taut; staple the fabric in place.*

3 *Arrange the ribbons, pull them taut, and tack them in place. Cut each ribbon to extend about 1" (2.5 cm) beyond the fabric on the back, then turn the board over and staple them in place.*

4 *Insert a tack at selected intersections, then hot glue a button to each tack. Toenail the finished board into the mirror frame. Add hanging hardware.*

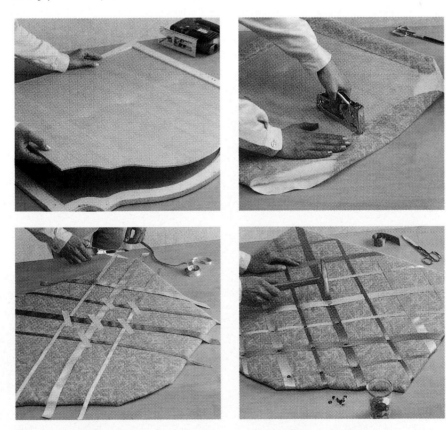

MATERIALS:

MIRROR FRAME • LATEX PAINT • ⅜" (9 MM) PLYWOOD • QUILT BATTING • FABRIC • RIBBONS
• TACKS • ANTIQUE BUTTONS • HOT GLUE • HANGING HARDWARE

FACE FORWARD

The value of an old painted piece can be destroyed by altering the finish in any way. But, especially if you want to store linens in an old cabinet or armoire, you may not want an exposed surface of peeling paint. Here's a quick and easy way to cover a rough interior surface without permanently altering the finish of the piece.

1▶ Remove the shelves and shelf supports. Cut a piece of foam board ¼" (6 mm) smaller than the length and width of the back of the cabinet. Use spray adhesive to attach an oversized piece of quilt batting to the foam board; trim the batting to fit.

2▶ Cut a piece of fabric, 4" (10 cm) larger than the foam board. Set the foam board—fleece side down—onto the wrong side of the fabric. Wrap the fabric around the foam board and glue it down as necessary. Press pieces of self-adhesive hook-and-loop tape onto the corners and sides of the back of the cabinet and the foam board. Position the foam board on the back of the cabinet, pressing it firmly to secure the hook-and-loop tape.

3▶ Wrap each shelf in fabric; glue the overlapped fabric at the back edge. Replace the shelf supports and shelves. Measure and cut foam board to fit the sections of the sides. Cover and install these side pieces, following the instructions above.

MATERIALS:

CABINET OR ARMOIRE • ACID-FREE FOAM BOARD
• ARCHIVIST'S SPRAY ADHESIVE • QUILT BATTING
• FABRIC • GLUE • SELF-ADHESIVE HOOK-AND-LOOP TAPE

LEAF YOUR SEAT

Tim and I love to use ordinary materials in extraordinary ways. Take this topiary. You start with an inexpensive chair—any size, shape, or condition. Add a little chicken wire and a few gardening supplies, and you've created a conversation piece that will improve as time goes by.

We planted the seat with baby's tears, which need bright light but should be kept out of the direct sun. To keep your topiary healthy, mist it regularly and water it carefully.

1 *Shape chicken wire around the back and legs of a wooden or metal chair. Use wire cutters to trim the chicken wire, and florist's wire to join the sections. Cover the seat with 6 mil plastic, then form the chicken wire into a shallow basket-like shape over it.*

2 *Cover the chicken wire with damp moss. Cut 3" (7.5 cm) pieces of florist's wire and bend each in half; use these to hold the moss in place. Wrap fishing line around the arms and legs, and tie the moss in place. Mix moisture-retention crystals into potting soil, and fill the seat area. Plant baby's tears (Soleirolia soleirolii) in the seat area.*

 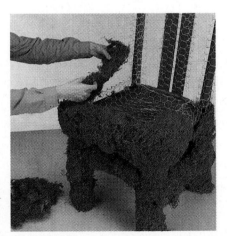

MATERIALS:

CHAIR • CHICKEN WIRE • SHEET MOSS • FISHING LINE • FLORIST'S WIRE
• 6 MIL PLASTIC • POTTING SOIL • MOISTURE-RETENTION CRYSTALS
• TRAILING PLANT SUCH AS BABY'S TEARS

ACCESSORIES

If furnishings are the wardrobe of a room, accessories are its jewelry. In the same way that the right earrings or necklace take a little black dress from plain to fancy, accessories spice things up. They add color, charm, and spirit to your rooms.

The best way to start accessorizing a flea-market-style home is with things you already have. Take those old photos out of their boxes or albums and frame them; buy or make a shadow box for that christening gown or first birthday dress; get out the kids' art projects and ask your folks if they still have yours packed away somewhere. When you use personal mementos and family photographs as accessories, your home becomes almost a living memory album, a daily reminder of your history and inspiration for your future.

If you're a collector, pull out your collections and give them places of honor throughout your home. Let their colors and textures provide the theme; add other accessories that complement them.

From there, move on to the unique, one-of-a-kind treasures that you dig up in your travels. Use these pieces in ways that please you—don't worry about what's in style or how other people decorate. A copper-roofed martin house stands on a pedestal in a corner of my dining room. You wouldn't believe how many friends have offered to help me put it in the yard, but there it stays— offbeat and charming. My friend Sally has an ancient barber's chair in her living room. Not very common, but entirely wonderful.

The best advice is simple: Have fun.

WHIMSY

Think of adding accessories as an opportunity to incorporate your favorite colors, to introduce unexpected patterns, and to include textures that please you. As you're scouting for accessories, remember that in the finished room you won't see one item at a time—each piece will always be seen in the context of its surroundings.

The sitting room at left includes a mixture of comforts and curiosities. I particularly appreciate the little birdhouse set on a candle pedestal, the leather gloves hung from pegs, and the framed print set low within the scene. Unusual touches like these reveal the personality and creative flair that set a room apart and make it special.

The unusual use of the birdcage shown above is another example of personal flair. Not many people would think of using a birdcage for a planter, but it's quite striking. Nor would many people make a lamp from a birdcage, but the one on page 118 is one of my favorite projects.

DETAILS

Accessories can also emphasize the details of the furnishings or structure of a room. The window treatment in the photo at left is made from a vintage table scarf. Folded at this angle, both its basic shape and the lines of its details complement the shapes of the leaded glass panes.

The accessories in the room above repeat the color scheme set by the rug. From the prints to the houseplants—even the tassel hanging from the side table—each accessory plays a part in producing a harmonious, polished look.

IMAGINATION

The collection of men's hats shown at left demonstrates the way accessories influence the feel of a room—their presence imparts such a masculine air to the surroundings. There was a time when a hat was as much a part of a man's clothing as his coat or shoes. John F. Kennedy, the first President to regularly appear bareheaded outdoors, is often credited (or blamed, depending on your point of view) with changing that long-standing tradition. Years later, there's a definite sense of romance associated with men's hats. They speak of their times and places, providing tangible evidence of a man's interests and habits.

The hats shown here give you a sense of an outdoorsman, an adventurer, perhaps a gentleman farmer. You have to wonder whether they all belonged to one person or were collected over time from a variety of sources. I like to imagine that they all belonged to a beloved relative and have been displayed as loving reminders of happy memories. Several years ago, I came across a collection of vintage clothing that marked the important occasions of an unknown woman's life. It was all there—from her christening gown to a dress made for her twenty-fifth wedding anniversary. Although it saddened me to see the collection being broken up, the whole set was far beyond my budget. Of all the pieces, the one that spoke to me the loudest was a wonderful creation of white lawn shaped by pin tucks and intricate stitches—the dress from her coming-out party. The previous year had been a time of struggle and change for me personally. My son had been seriously injured in a car accident, and I'd gone through a devastating divorce. After months of dwelling in grief and disbelief, I'd begun to build a new life and a stronger, bolder sense of myself; the dress felt like a symbol of my emergence from that hell. It now hangs on my bedroom door as a reminder of how far I've come. I often imagine the memories it held for my unknown friend.

The room setting at right illustrates that there are many ways to meet a challenge. One accessory—the framed print hanging in the center of the window—anchors the composition. Without it, the desk and chair would appear to be floating in space in front of the window.

The print also sets the color theme for the entire room. The black and gold of the frame and the neutral tones of the print are repeated by the furnishings and other accessories. Even the old-fashioned fan in the corner has been selected to contribute a certain feeling to the scene.

SASHAYING AROUND

As you walk through any flea market, you come to understand that no matter how odd the piece or category, there are people who collect it. Political buttons, flying pigs, vintage Elvis on black velvet—it's all there.

It seems that display space is always at a premium for collectors. This mirrored shadow box made from an old window sash might be just the ticket for a collection you hold dear.

1 Measure each side of the window sash (old windows are not likely to be square). Cut 1 × 6 (2.5 × 15 cm) lumber to match the top and bottom of the sash. Subtract 1½" (38 mm) from the length of the sides and cut 1 × 6s (2.5 × 15 cm) to match. Form the pieces into a frame, lapping the joints as shown in the diagram at right. Prime and paint the frame to match the sash. (We used a base coat, crackle medium, and top coat.)

2 Measure the inside dimensions of the frame and have a mirror cut to size. Cut a piece of ½" (12 mm) plywood to match the outside dimensions of the frame. Prime and paint the plywood. Screw the plywood to the back of the frame with the painted side on the outside. Use construction adhesive to glue the mirror to the plywood, inside the frame.

3 Cut a divider to fit between the top and bottom of the frame and a shelf for every horizontal muntin. Prime and paint these pieces. Set the window sash over the frame and align the divider and shelves with the muntins. Mark their locations, then install the pieces. Attach pairs of mending plates to the sides of the sash and then to the frame, securing the sash to the frame. Add hanging hardware.

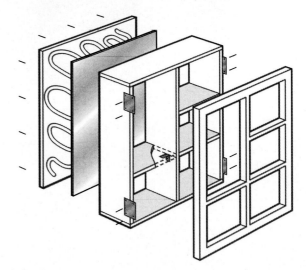

MATERIALS:

MULTI-PANED WINDOW SASH • 1 × 6 LUMBER (2.5 × 15 CM)
• WOOD GLUE • PRIMER AND PAINT TO MATCH SASH • 4D FINISH NAILS
• MIRROR, CUSTOM CUT • ½" (12 MM) PLYWOOD • CONSTRUCTION ADHESIVE
• 1½" (38 MM) GALVANIZED DECK SCREWS • ANGLE IRON (4 PER SHELF)
• ½" (12 MM) WOOD SCREWS • FLAT MENDING PLATES (4)

GREAT BACK UP

What causes the fascination little boys have with taking things apart? My nephew, Brendan, once convinced my son, Evan, to help him disassemble an entire wooden swingset because it interfered with their plans. Brendan was about eight and Evan about six at the time, and we couldn't believe how close they came to accomplishing the task before the adults caught on. In the next few years, they went on to take apart bicycles, roller blades—even a lawn mower.

Taking a chair apart for this unique project is a compara-tive breeze. The chair back frames the wreath, making each seem more interesting than it otherwise would be.

1 ▸ *Loosen the blocks holding the seat in place and remove the seat. Pry away the side braces. Mark cutting lines and cut off the legs, using a jig saw. Touch up the finish, or paint the chair back.*

2 ▸ *Attach a brass hook to the wall; make sure you hit a stud or use hollow wall anchors. Set the chair back onto the hook and then suspend a wreath from a ribbon also hung from the hook.*

MATERIALS:
WOODEN CHAIR • BRASS HOOK • RIBBON • WREATH

JUST HANGING AROUND

Architectural salvage places are filled with collections of intricate and beautiful doorknobs and escutcheon plates. Incomplete passage sets aren't very expensive, but what do you do with them? Here are two good ideas.

Hanger board: *Drill pilot holes in a piece of reclaimed lumber and install a hanger bolt in each. Remove the stems from the doorknobs, either by unscrewing the knob, loosening the set screw, or cutting the stem with a hacksaw. Attach each knob to a hanger bolt, and then add hanging hardware to the back of the board.*

Door Hanger: *Remove the stem from the doorknob as described above. Mark and drill a pilot hole, and install a hanger bolt on a door or wall. If you're installing the bolt on a wall, be sure you hit a stud or use appropriate hardware. Attach the escutcheon, then screw the doorknob onto the hanger bolt.*

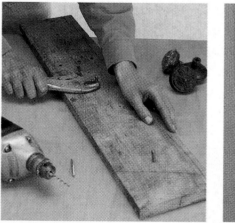 

MATERIALS:

DOORKNOBS AND ESCUTCHEONS • HANGER BOLTS (1 PER KNOB)
• RECLAIMED LUMBER • HANGING HARDWARE

THROUGH THE LOOKING GLASS

Remember the door in *Alice in Wonderland*? The one marked "Open Me"? Old doors always feel as if they're asking to be opened, as though there will be something exciting or fun or beautiful on the other side. By replacing part of the center panel with a mirror and adding a plant shelf, you can turn an old door into an elegant accent that invites friends and family into a room.

1 ▶ *Remove the center panels from the top third of the door. (Drill starter holes, make cuts with a jig saw, and then pull the pieces from the frame.) Restore or refinish the door, if you wish.*

2 ▶ *Have a mirror cut to fit the opening. Set the mirror into the opening and secure it with glazier's points. Drill pilot holes and attach a shelf bracket to the door, centered just below the opening. Set the shelf into place.*

MATERIALS:

SALVAGED DOOR • MIRROR, CUSTOM CUT
• SHELF BRACKET • GLAZIER'S POINTS

JUST A FRAME-UP

Although it's made from little more than lumber from a discarded pallet, this frame is perfect for an old photo, such as the one seen here of Tim's mother in the arms of her father. You can make interesting frames from salvaged molding, trim pieces, or barnwood as well.

When I first got interested in making frames from salvaged lumber, I was afraid it might prove to be complicated. But then my dad taught me the easy trick we used to reinforce these joints. It's a simplified version of a technique used in fine woodworking—just right for anyone with basic skills and tools. (Thanks, Dad.)

1 *Cut a length of lumber that will accommodate the frame you plan to make. Using a router and a piloted rabbet bit set at ¼" (6 mm), cut a rabbet down the length of the wood, along what will be the frame's inside edge.*

2 *Cut four pieces, mitering the ends at 45°. Apply polyurethane glue to the edges and assemble the joints. Band the frame together while the glue dries.*

3 *Cut six circles of ¼" (6 mm) plywood, using a 1" (2.5 cm) hole saw. Use a 1" (2.5 cm) spade bit to drill two holes centered along each joint. Glue one plywood circle into each hole to secure the joints.*

MATERIALS:

SALVAGED LUMBER • POLYURETHANE GLUE • SCRAP PLYWOOD

COMPOSITION

Accessories have more impact when they're arranged so you see them as a group, rather than as random objects. This idea is carried out in both rooms shown here. The pieces are not only grouped, they've been integrated into the scene.

Arranging accessories is a lot like composing a still life, and you can follow some of the same principles. The area that you're accessorizing basically acts as the background, and the goal is to create an interesting balance between the accessories and the spaces that surround them.

The first thing to do is collect all the objects. Whether you're creating a new arrangement or significantly changing an existing one, put all the pieces on the floor or a table and spend some time studying the various sizes and shapes you plan to use. When I create a new arrangement, I usually scatter the things around me and look at them until something speaks to me as a starting point. Typically you'll want to put the largest objects in the back, so it often makes sense to start with those. Keep trying out possible arrangements until something jells. Don't worry—you'll recognize it when it happens.

Be careful not to crowd the arrangement. It's a good idea to overlap a few pieces, but make sure you can see each object clearly. Just as in a painting, you want certain elements to lead the eye into and around the image you're creating. In the bedroom shown at right, the twig basket in the upper right corner points down and into the scene, the branches arranged in the vase at center point out and down toward the chaise, and the corner of the dresser scarf leads your eye toward the small table. Even the illumination patterns of the lamps have been taken into consideration here—look at the way the shadows play a part in the overall picture.

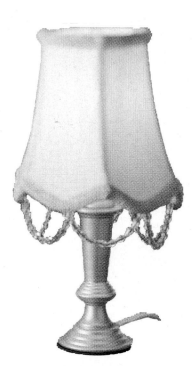

When Tim and I are working on a project design and I start fretting over the placement of one element or another, he reminds me of what he calls the "rule of thirds." That's his favorite way of describing a pleasing spatial relationship.

Boiled down to its essence, it means that if you're going to overlap two objects, do it by about a third. If you're going to stagger two objects, place the top of one about a third of the way down from the top of the other. There are more complex theories and rules for composition, but you can't go wrong by following Tim's rule of thirds.

SIMPLICITY

When you're arranging accessories, let their character guide you. With highly detailed accessories, simplicity is the key. In the bedroom shown at right, the simple setting allows the details of the ceramic lamp to shine; the mirror adds depth to the arrangement.

The spare lines of the hutch in the gathering room shown above are perfect for the collection of ceramics and china displayed there. These colorful accessories blend well with the worn, painted finish, with the other furnishings in the room, and with one another.

VERTICAL SPACE

It's important to take advantage of vertical space, especially in small rooms. You can do this by finding display pieces that allow you to stack accessories. The cabinet in the vignette shown at left was originally used as a medicine chest; it now houses a charming collection of children's shoes. The vertical element of this display is emphasized by the way the shoe collection spills out onto the table and by the varied heights of the lamps and the stack of doll trunks.

In the small sitting room shown above, a lodge-pole ladder rises in the corner, offering a home to a collection of Native American rugs and blankets. The positioning of the floor lamp and the framed art help draw your eye up and into the corner, completing the illusion of greater space.

GREAT WRITE UPS

Between cell phones, voice mail, e-mail, and synched-up PDAs, there's no shortage of ways to communicate these days. But still, I love to find a note from one of my kids when I walk in the door at night, and they seem to like finding notes from me. Whether it's a reminder about the evening's plans, a suggestion about dinner, or just "Hi there. I love you," handwritten notes have a personal feeling that no electronic means of communication can touch.

By adding a couple coats of blackboard paint and some coat hooks, you can turn a salvaged door panel into an attractive, functional message center. Then all you need is chalk and something to say.

1 *Cut the door panel to size. If you like, remove the old finish and sand the entire piece. Mask off the center panel, then stain and apply a finish to the rails and stiles.*

2 *When the finish is completely dry, mask off the rails and styles, and apply several coats of blackboard paint to the center panel.*

3 *Add brass hooks along the bottom rail, and an escutcheon and doorknob to the stile on one side.*

MATERIALS:

PANEL DOOR • BLACKBOARD PAINT • BRASS HOOKS (3)
• DOORKNOB AND ESCUTCHEON PLATE

ADORABLE

My grandma stored the fruits and vegetables she canned in what we called "the cave." In some parts of the country, these outdoor, underground pantries were referred to as root cellars. By any name, there's little need for such stor-age areas these days. Even so, you can recall the ambiance of that era by replacing a standard pantry door with a salvaged screen door. Add some shelf edging, and even everyday items will look special.

1▸ *Measure the pantry's opening. Mark cutting lines on the screen door, check it against the opening, then cut it to fit. Touch up the paint or finish as necessary.*

2▸ *Mark the outline of two hinges, then chisel out mortises, each about ⅛" (3 mm) deep.*

3▸ *Position the hinge hardware within the mortise, and attach it to the door, using the screws provided.*

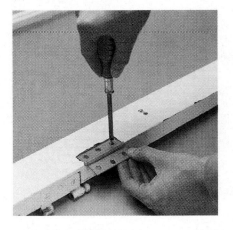

4▸ *Position the door and make sure it's level. Mark and drill pilot holes, then shim the door into position and drive the screws into the cabinet. On the front of the door, attach a door pull or handle.*

MATERIALS:

SCREEN DOOR • PAINT OR STAIN AS NECESSARY
• HINGES (2) • DOOR PULL OR HANDLE

PICTURE THIS

Tim's daughter, Molly, keeps pictures of her friends all over her room. Tucking her into bed one night, Tim caught sight of one of her collections and was struck by the idea for this project. It's terrific—inexpensive, easy to do, and just the kind of thing a teenage girl loves.

1▸*Choose a crystal doorknob that has a flat or concave face. Loosen the set screw and remove the stem from the knob.*

2▸*Cut lengths of silver solder; form a spiral at the end of each piece. Gather the solder pieces and arrange them much as you would a handful of flowers. Wrap a piece of fine-gauge wire around the ends to hold the pieces together. Use hot glue to secure the solder in the handle of the doorknob.*

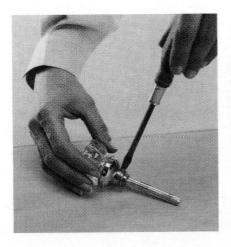 

MATERIALS:

CRYSTAL DOORKNOB • SILVER SOLDER
• 16-GAUGE (1.5 MM) WIRE • HOT GLUE

DRESSED UP & SHOWING OFF

Unlike most, my children arrived fully clothed. I've always wanted to do something special with the clothing they were each wearing when we greeted them at the adoption agency, but nothing ever seemed quite right. The moment I came across this domed-glass frame, I knew it was the answer.

It's a shame we no longer have the matching green ribbon that was scotch-taped to her little bald head, but I love this display of the dress my Katie was wearing the first time I held her. You might want to show off a christening gown or baby bonnet from your own family, or a treasure you've found in your travels.

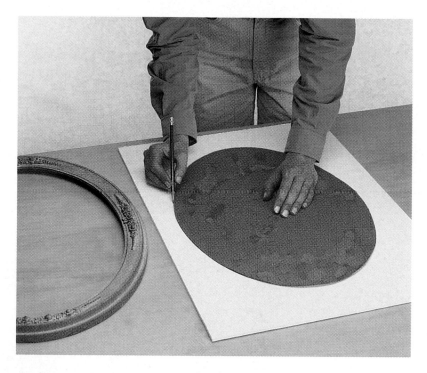

1ᐅ Disassemble the frame. Using the original as a template, cut a foam board. (If the original isn't available, cut a board ¼" [6 mm] smaller than the frame opening.)

2ᐅ Cut a piece of fabric 2" (5 cm) larger than the mounting board. Cover the foam board with spray adhesive, then wrap the fabric around it. Tape the edges of the fabric to the back of the board.

3ᐅ Attach the items to the mounting board. Support clothing with three or four strategically placed hand stitches, then bring the threads to the back, tie the tails, and secure them. Use silicone glue to hold other items in place. Set the mounting board in the frame and insert ¾" (19 mm) brads into the center of each side, then

the top and bottom. Insert additional brads at about 2" (5 cm) intervals. Cover the frame back with brown paper, using double-stick transfer tape. Replace the hanging hardware.

MATERIALS:

FRAME WITH DOMED GLASS • ACID-FREE FOAM BOARD
• ARCHIVIST'S SPRAY ADHESIVE • FRAMER'S TAPE
• SILICONE GLUE • ¾" (19 MM) BRADS
• BROWN PAPER • LINEN FRAMER'S TAPE
• HANGING HARDWARE

THYME IN A BOTTLE

Several years ago my Christmas gift to my best friend was an old bottle that once held specimen plants gathered in 1904 for Kew Gardens. As a master gardener, he appreciated its history. I loved its mystique. Most old bottles carry that sense of history and mystery—stories of where they have been and how they have been used. Frequently found in strik-ing colors and interesting shapes, they can be put to use throughout the house.

Oil lamp: *Fill an old bottle with lamp oil. Arrange silk or dried flowers in the oil, using a chopstick or a knitting needle to compose the flowers in a pleasing arrangement. Thread a length of lamp wick through a glass or metal bead, position the wick in the oil, and settle the bead in the mouth of the bottle.*

Oil dispenser: *Fill a bottle with oil and add fresh herbs. Arrange the herbs as described above. Add a pour spout or cap.*

MATERIALS:
OLD BOTTLES • LAMP WICK • GLASS OR METAL BEAD
• FLOWERS • HERBS • OLIVE OIL • LAMP OIL • POURING SPOUTS

ILLUMINATION

Candles, lamps, and chandeliers are very valuable accessories. You can use lighting to play tricks that improve the shape and proportion of a room, highlight an interesting detail, or disguise an ugly one. To make a ceiling look higher, use floor lamps or wall sconces that throw the light upward. On the other hand, keeping most of the lighting at lower levels reduces the seeming height of a room. Positioning lamps or candles so they're reflected in mirrors at the end or side of a room makes the room appear to be deeper or wider, depending on their placement.

If a room includes valuable art or vintage fabrics, be especially careful about the type and placement of the lighting—some types of lighting can cause fading or discoloration. Many lighting stores have specialists who can give you advice and guidance on this subject.

For most circumstances, the following guidelines will produce an effective lighting scheme: The lower edge of the shade on a table lamp should be at eye level when you're seated—about 38 to 42" (95 to 105 cm) above the floor. The lower edge of the shade on floor lamps should be about 40 to 49" (100 to 123 cm) from the floor. Taller lamps used for reading should be positioned 15" (38 cm) to the side and 20" (50 cm) behind the center of the book when you're reading. Chandeliers should be suspended 34 to 36" (85 to 90 cm) above the surface of the table in dining areas, and well above a person's height in hallways and other walking areas.

The table lamp in the bedroom shown above bathes the rest of the tabletop accessories in a cozy glow. You can use colored shades or specialty light bulbs to produce that type of warmth. Again, a lighting specialist can help you find the right shade and bulb to create the effect you want.

Back in the days when candles were extremely expensive, mirror-backed sconces and mirror-lined walls were used to reflect and multiply their precious light. It still works today. In the table setting shown at right, light is bounced off and reflected from several surfaces and finishes—the table surface, the glass beads, and the glassware reflect the glow of the candles and increase their visual weight.

MOOD

The shade or fitting you select has a significant impact on the quality of light produced by a lamp or light fixture. In the hallway shown at left, the cone-shaped shade casts light downward, a nice way to light a collection of tabletop accessories. The opaque glass of the nautilus-shell shade diffuses the light to produce a warm glow and cast interesting shadows.

In the living room shown above, the fanciful shades reinforce the lively mood set by the fabrics and other accessories. During the day, this room has plenty of natural light. At night, the exposed windows provide a reflective surface for the lamp light. On the mantle, candles are set in front of a mirror to multiply their impact.

When you're selecting shades, keep in mind the style and shape of the lamp, the tone of the room, and the effect you're trying to create with each particular lamp.

HIGHLIGHTS

Lighting also can draw your eye to special accessories or create points of interest within a display. In the living room shown at right, most of the Native American art pieces have matte surfaces. By adding a few accessories with reflective surfaces, the collector created highlights that make the collection appear even more appealing. By the way, this room offers another example of the way mirrors can be used to play with light—look at the way the crystal chandelier and the lamp in the background are reflected and multiplied by the mirror.

It's a very different setting, but the bedroom above also illustrates the effective use of light and reflective surfaces. The beads adorning the Buddha, the crystals and shells on the frames—even the satin embroidery on the shawl draped over the chair—catch your eye and demand attention. Just like magpies, people are drawn to and cheered by shiny things. Don't be afraid to add a bit of sparkle to your mix.

ALL THE TEA IN CHINA

My grandmother, master gardener and lover of dishes, got me started collecting teacups. I can still feel the pride with which I presented the latest prize from my travels and the way she beamed as she assured me that this was the prettiest one ever. If you share our obsession, you'll appreciate this lamp.

1▶ *Drill a ½" (12 mm) hole in the center of each cup and saucer. Support each piece in a bucket of sand; use a glass and tile bit and drill slowly. Stack the teacups and measure them. Purchase a threaded nipple that will accommodate the stack and leave about ½" (12 mm) at the top; purchase one 1" (2.5 cm) coupler for each inch of the nipple. (Allowing about 1" [2.5 cm] between cups, we used a 13" [33 cm] nipple and 13 couplers.) Slide a lock washer and a hex nut onto one end of the threaded nipple. Insert the nipple into the hole of the lamp base. Place a rubber washer over the nipple.*

2▶ *Set the first cup and saucer in place, add a rubber washer and a brass washer, then screw four brass couplers onto the threaded nipple. Add a brass washer and a rubber washer, the second cup, and a second set of washers; repeat to add the third cup. Screw on four more couplers, and top the assembly with a threaded brass washer, a harp, and another threaded brass washer.*

3▶ *Attach a socket cap to the nipple. Insert a lamp cord through the base and the nipple. Tie the split ends of the wire in an underwriter's knot, connect them to the lamp socket, and assemble the socket (see page 32). Add a lampshade and, if desired, a finial.*

MATERIALS:

CHINA CUPS AND SAUCERS (3 SETS) • THREADED NIPPLE • LOCK WASHER (1) • HEX NUT (1) • 1" (2.5 CM) BRASS COUPLERS (ONE FOR EACH INCH OF THREADED NIPPLE) • BRASS WASHERS (6) • RUBBER WASHERS (6) • LAMP BASE • HARP • SOCKET CAP • LAMP SOCKET • LAMPSHADE

LATE NIGHT FLIGHT

Especially during the Victorian era, birds were common pets. There are plenty of old, ornate birdcages available, and it's remarkably easy to convert them into lamp bases. A cage with an interesting shape and intricate details makes a particularly good choice for this project.

1 ▶ *If the cage doesn't have feet, add small blocks or dowels to act as a base. If necessary, drill a hole through the top of the birdcage. (We had to first cut off a knurl.) Insert a brass pipe threaded on each end. Above the wires on the bottom of the cage, add a threaded nut and a fender washer; below the wires add a fender washer, a lock nut, and a threaded nut. Tighten the threaded nuts to hold the pipe in place.*

2 ▶ *Add a threaded knurl nut and then a harp to the top of the brass pipe; attach the socket cap. Pull the lamp cord through the brass pipe and into the socket cap. Tie the split ends of the wire in an underwriter's knot, connect them to the lamp socket, and assemble the socket (see page 32). Add a lampshade and, if you like, a finial.*

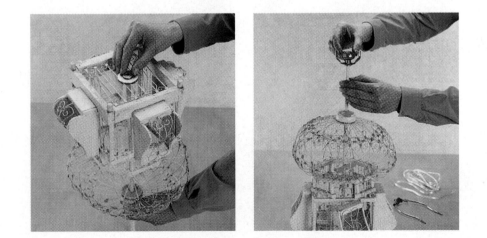

MATERIALS:
BIRDCAGE • THREADED NUTS (2) • FENDER WASHERS (2) • LOCK NUT
• THREADED KNURL NUT • THREADED BRASS PIPE • SOCKET CAP • SOCKET
• LAMP CORD • LAMPSHADE

CATCH A FALLING STAR

Any kind of light in a jar reminds me of lightning bugs. These magical creatures have entertained generations of children, including my cousins and me. We didn't know or care what made them light up; we just loved to see them hovering above the grass, sparkling like miniature stars.

Many of you also probably spent summer evenings chasing lightning bugs through the grass or woods, carrying a jar in one hand and a lid punched with holes in the other. If so, filling a few old-fashioned jars with candles is an easy way to evoke happy memories. And if you've never caught lightning bugs, maybe it's time!

1▸ *Cut two equal-length pieces of wire. With the end of the first wire extending 3 to 4" (7.5 to 10 cm) past the rim of the jar, form a series of vertical loops that reach three-quarters of the way up and half-way around the jar. Cut the wire, again letting the end extend 3 to 4" (7.5 to 10 cm) past the rim of the jar. Shape the second wire around the other half of the jar in the same way. Bend the ends of the loops down to support the bottom of the jar. Twist the ends of the extensions together, connecting the two sets of loops.*

2▸ *Form a hanging loop and attach it to the twisted sections. Fill the jar with sand and/or decorative stones and add votive candles.*

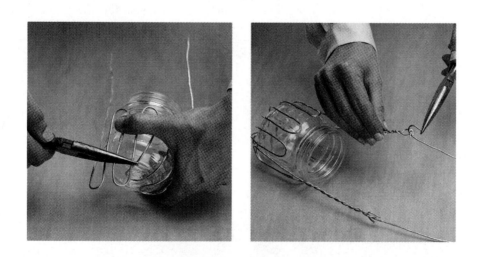

MATERIALS:

12-GAUGE (2 MM) GALVANIZED WIRE • HALF-PINT OR PINT CANNING JARS
• SAND • DECORATIVE STONES • VOTIVE CANDLES

LETTING YOUR LIGHT SHINE

Working on this book, Tim and I have come to believe that almost anything can be made into a lamp. But when a great deal of imagination has gone into the base, I just hate to top it with a plain shade. Here are a few ideas that will help you embellish shades for your favorite lamps—ones you've bought as well as those you've created from found treasures.

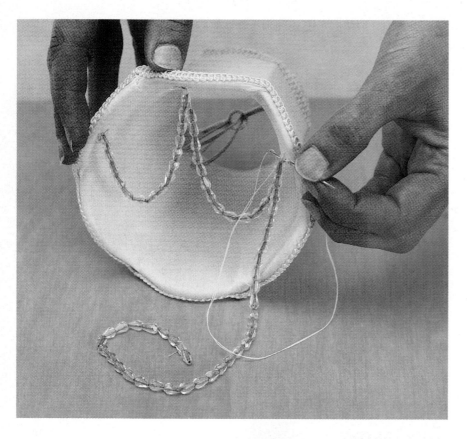

Scalloped shade: *Thread a medium-sized needle with dental floss. Leaving a long tail inside the shade, make two or three stitches to secure one end of the bead string to the center of one of the shade's scallops. Work your way around the shade, stitching the beads in the center of each scallop. End the last stich inside the shade and tie a knot in the floss. If you like, glue a button to cover the stitches on each scallop.*

Feathered shade: *Hot glue bands of feathers around a simple shade. Add a row of ribbon to the top and the bottom.*

Bell-shaped shade: *Hot glue beaded fringe to the lower edge of a bell-shaped shade.*

MATERIALS:

ASSORTED LAMP SHADES • STRINGS OF BEADS
• DENTAL FLOSS • ANTIQUE BUTTONS
• HOT GLUE • FEATHER TRIM
• BEADED FRINGE

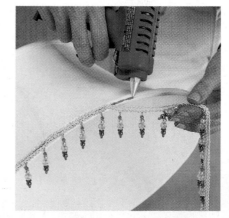

MASS

In the sitting room shown above, we see the power of massed accessories. The scene has much more impact than you'd otherwise get from a few pieces of china and a handful of flowers. Even the pile of pillows in the corner basket contributes to the lux-
urious, genteel image.

In the entertainment area shown at right, the entire room is changed by several handfuls of flowers. What a great idea—
collect several dozen small, inexpensive, clear glass vases. When you want to make a big spash, fill each vase with one or two
stems of simple flowers. Arrange groups of vases to produce the illusion of a room-sized bouquet.

COLLECTIONS

The most interesting collections are comprised of unique, sometimes even one-of-a-kind items that have a personal history or special meaning to the person who collects them. The charming living room at left is a colorful jumble of the odd and the unusual, including many toys and novelties. Looking at these displays, you can just feel the joy the collector took in assembling them.

Some old pieces are so strongly tied to family memories that they seem irreplaceable—it's the kind of thing that's often been known to lead to hard feelings among family members. My mother came up with a brilliant way of sharing one plate among four people.

After my grandmother's death, Mom inherited an amber Depression-glass plate that her mother got at dish night at the movies. (During the Depression, dishes were offered as incentives for people to part with their hard-earned cash for mere entertainment.) Many years later Mom still treasured the plate, although she had long forgotten the movie associated with it.

There was, unfortunately, only one plate and four of us who cherished the memories it represented—my mother, my sister, my brother, and me. One day at a farm auction, Mom happened to notice an identical plate being sold. She bought that one and, over time, found two more just like it. The next time we were all together, she put the original plate and the three impostors in a stack and shuffled them around until even she no longer knew which one was which. She then invited each of us to select the plate we believed to be Grandma's.

This clever trick allowed each of us to believe that we ended up with Grandma's plate. My plate—the real one, by the way—now stands in a glass-front kitchen cabinet above my pantry, where I can see and enjoy it every day.

No matter how you have acquired your special treasures, display them proudly. Family heirlooms and found objects alike put your personal signature on your home and make it uniquely your own.

FLORAL ACCENTS

Fresh flowers instantly brighten a room, particularly those that have neutral or pale color schemes. Elaborate blossoms are suited to ornate vases, such as the one displayed on the bedroom dresser above. Simple flowers, such as the tulips displayed on the mantle at right, are best suited to vases with clean lines and simple shapes. Even a relatively small collection of these vases creates an elegant impression. Here, only a handful of flowers is required to complete the scene.

Don't restrict yourself to actual vases. Almost any container that can hold water can be used to display flower arrangements—jars, buckets, pitchers, tin cans, tea kettles, or watering cans, to name just a few. The more imaginative, the better. Most such containers can be adapted to hold houseplants as well. Just be sure to provide adequate drainage.

CONTAINERS

Flower arrangements are wonderful, but there are other great ways to throw spots of color into a room. I'm not sure which adds more to the kitchen at left, the zinnias or the basket of vegetables. Even the jars of home-canned vegetables do their part. (If you want to see a beautiful display of home-canned vegetables, take a look at the pantry project on page 102. My Aunt Donna canned some of those vegetables, and let me assure you—they taste just as good as they look.)

We've seen that unusual containers add character to a room, but so do interesting materials. In the windowsill above, a bowl of pomegranates and a wire basket filled with dried berries provide color as well as a definite sense of personality.

Be alert for new ways to use containers you already have. A friend of mine planted an herb garden in an old enamel wash pan. At mealtime, she adds a couple iron candlehold-ers on plant stakes to turn the herb garden into a lovely centerpiece. At other times she keeps the garden in a sunny spot on the kitchen counter, well within reach as she cooks.

URNING YOUR KEEP

Antique garden ornaments have become prize possessions, and if you've been lucky enough to find an old urn in good condition, you probably want to show it off. That may mean using it in unexpected ways, such as inside the house. An urn would look terrific in an entryway, filled with arrangements that change with the seasons. Try seed or moss or feather balls twined with fairy lights.

Fill the urn with seasonal greens and ornaments. We suggest pine boughs and mercury balls for winter, straw and gourds for fall. If your urn is the right size, you could turn it into a side table by topping it with a piece of glass that overhangs the lip by approximately 2" (5 cm).

MATERIALS:

GARDEN URN • GREENERY
• SEASONAL ORNAMENTS

PAILS OF POSIES

Tim's mom kept a garden that stretched 80 feet (24 m) long and 25 feet (8 m) wide. Her garden produced the usual array of fruits and vegetables, but certain areas were designated for flowers, and the back row was always reserved for gladiolas. Tim remembers carrying enormous buckets of flowers up to the house at the end of a day's gardening; he also remembers the smell of flowers throughout the house.

Even if you don't have a cutting garden, you can fill your home with the fragrance of buckets of flowers.

1▶Poke six or eight holes in a cake tin or aluminum pie pan, using an awl or nail set. Set a pan (upside down) into the bottom of each bucket. Cover each pan with a piece of landscape fabric and a 2" (5 cm) layer of pea gravel. Add potting soil and plants.

2▶Install a large hook in the ceiling—use hardware designed for the load and be sure you hit a joist. Drill a ½"-diameter (12 mm) hole a few inches from each end of a 10" (25 cm) piece of a hardwood 1 × 2 (2.5 × 5 cm). Run a rope around the pulley and thread one end through each hole in the 1 × 2 (2.5 × 5 cm). Suspend the pulley from a chain attached to the ceiling hook, then tie one end of the rope to each bucket.

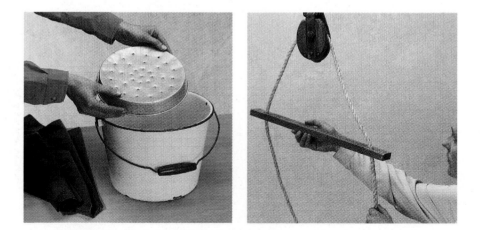

MATERIALS:

BUCKETS • CAKE TINS • LANDSCAPE FABRIC • GRAVEL
• LIGHTWEIGHT POTTING SOIL • PLANTS • CEILING HOOK (RATED FOR AT LEAST
25 POUNDS [11 KG]) • SCRAP OF HARDWOOD 1 × 2 (2.5 × 5 CM)
• ROPE • PULLEY • BRASS CHAIN

AFTERWORD

Not long ago I rearranged my dining room to feature a display of my grandmother's dishes. Although I inherited these dishes, it didn't happen in the way you might expect….

Hazel Jackson Farris, my father's mother, married young, during the Depression. Grandma's family had been relatively comfortable, and she inherited many family treasures—her grandmother's china, linens, and assorted housewares.

Early in their marriage, she and her husband, Floyd, worked as migrant farmers, picking strawberries in Sarcoxie, Missouri. A family tragedy suddenly forced Grandma and Grandpa to return home to Illinois. They could take only what they could fit into the trunk of their car, so Grandpa built a wooden box, packed Grandma's china and other precious bits and pieces into it, and convinced the landowner to keep the box in the barn until the next spring, when he planned to return for it.

Life intervened, as it has a way of doing, and Grandpa never went back for the box. Grandma never got over it. To the end of her life, when she couldn't find a dish or a glass or a sentimental memento—anything at all, really—she would mutter darkly, "I probably left that in the box in Sarcoxie." In fact, the last words she ever spoke were about that box. In her euology, one of her sons told this story and estimated that the box must have been roughly the size of a boxcar to have held all the things she was sure were lost in it.

Grandma left $500 to each of her ten surviving grandchildren. When I learned of this, I knew immediately what to do with that money. With great joy, I bought the most old-fashioned, grandmotherly set of china I could find. To me, they are my grandmother's dishes, and I like to believe that Grandma knows that, together, we reclaimed them.

My point is this: Whether you inherited your heirlooms directly or created them in some way, surround yourself with them. Recall and rejoice in their memories or imagine their stories.

jlf

$\mathcal{I}$NDEX

Index (cont.)

PHOTOGRAPHERS

Derek Fell's Horticultural Library
Pipersville, PA
©Derek Fell: pp. 125, 130

Gloria Gale
Overland Park, KS
Gloria Gale with the following
photographers:
©Ron Anderson: p. 66;
©Bill Mathews: pp. 38, 51, 78, 83, 94,
   97, 111, 124;
©Brad Simmons p. 98

Susan Gillmore
Esto Photographics
Mamaroneck, NY
©Susan Gillmore/Esto: pp. 35, 41

Robert Kern
Fair Lawn, NJ
©Robert Kern: p. 128

Balthazar Korab, Ltd.
Troy, MI
©Balthazar Korab: pp. 19B, 63

Karen Melvin
Architectural Stock Images, Inc.
Minneapolis, MN
©Karen Melvin: pp. 10, 65, 77,
   82, 112, 115
© Karen Melvin for the following:
Sandy Buchholtz, Designer:
   pp. 14, 95, 99, 110, 114;
Alison Drake Interior Design and
   Randall Kipp Architect: pp. 50, 81, 113;
Earl Gutnick, Designer p. 55
Jerilyn Hansen, Designer: pp. 53, 97;

Méli-Mélo French Decor/Tami Roth:
   p. 39;
Sotera Tschetter & Ann Marsden,
   Designers: pp. 5, 11, 54, 67;
Judy Onofrio, Artist: pp. 19T, 126

Jerry Pavia Photography, Inc.
Bonners Ferry, ID
©Jerry Pavia: p. 74

Greg Premru Photography
Boston, MA
©Greg Premru: pp. 6, 12, 62, 128

Eric Roth Photography
Topsfield, MA
©Eric Roth: p. 80

Kate Roth Photography
Chicago, IL
©Kate Roth: p. 131

Brad Simmons
Esto Photographics
Mamaroneck, NY
©Brad Simmons/Esto: pp. 36, 37

John Ferro Sims
Garden Picture Library
London, United Kingdom
©John Ferro Sims/
Garden Picture Library: p. 52

Steven Wooster
Garden Picture Library
London, United Kingdom
©Steven Wooster/
Garden Picture Library: p. 79

CONTRIBUTORS

We would like to thank the following stores and companies for their generous support.

April Cornell
3565 Galleria
Edina, MN 55435
952-836-0830
www.aprilcornell.com

Apropylis
1520 East 46th Street
Minneapolis, MN 55407
612-827-1974
rajtarprod@worldnet.att.net

Crescent Moon
58 So. Hamline (@ Grand)
St. Paul, MN 55105
651-690-9630

The Guilded Salvage Antiques
1315 NE Tyler St.
Minneapolis, MN 55413
612-789-1680

Old World Antiques
4911 Excelsior Blvd.
St. Louis Park, MN 55416
952-929-1638

Past Lives
1787 St. Clair Ave.
St. Paul, MN 55105
651-696-9233
www.pastlivesinc.com

Smith & Hawken
3564 Galleria
Edina, MN 55435
952-285-1110
www.smithandhawken.com

Squire House Gardens
1129 Grand Avenue
St. Paul, MN 55105
651-665-0142

CREDITS

CREATIVE PUBLISHING international

President/CEO: Michael Eleftheriou
Vice President/Publisher: Linda Ball
Vice President/Retail Sales & Marketing:
Kevin Haas

Copyright © 2001
Creative Publishing international, Inc.
5900 Green Oak Drive
Minnetonka, MN 55343
1-800-328-3895
www.creativepub.com

Printed by Quebecor World
10 9 8 7 6 5 4 3 2 1

Executive Editor: Bryan Trandem
Editorial Director: Jerri Farris
Creative Director: Tim Himsel
Managing Editor: Michelle Skudlarek

Authors: Jerri Farris, Tim Himsel
Editor: Barbara Harold
Project Manager: Tracy Stanley
Copy Editor: Tracy Stanley
Assisting Art Directors: Kari Johnston, Russ Kuepper
Mac Designer: Joe Fahey
Stock Photo Editors: Julie Caruso, Angie Hartwell
Technical Photo Stylist: Julie Caruso
Creative Photo Stylist: John Rajtar
Prop Stylist: Paul Gorton
Additional Project Design: Terrie Myers

Studio Services Manager: Marcia Chambers
Photographers: Tate Carlson, Andrea Rugg
Scene Shop Carpenters: Scott Ashfield, Dan Widerski
Director, Production Services: Kim Gerber
Illustrator: Jan-Willem Boer
Author Portraits by: Andrea Rugg
Cover Photograph by:
Karen Melvin for Roddy Turner, Designer